DIESELS IN THE HIGHLANDS

BR DIESELS

IN
THE HIGHLANDS

G. WEEKES

D. BRADFORD BARTON LIMITED

Frontispiece: amid typical scenery on the Kyle of Lochalsh line, one of the dependable BR - Sulzer Class 25s from Inverness depot heads up the climb of Strath Bran, west of Loch Luichart, with the mid-day Inverness - Kyle train, May 1974. Something like fifteen miles of adverse gradients are ahead up through Achanalt and Achnasheen to Luib summit (646') before the run down to the coast. Although the general tendency is a climb to the westward, the natural gradients on this section of line are undulating in a way rare in Britain, with a hundred yards or so up, followed by another short distance down following the rise and fall of the ground in the style of a colonial railway line. From the cab of a diesel, the appearance is said to look almost like a fairground switchback. Note the salmon ladder in the rocky bed of the river close alongside the line.   [K. R. Pirt]

© copyright D. Bradford Barton 1976   6711/3 NB   ISBN 0 85153 241 1

printed in Great Britain by H. E. Warne Ltd, London and St. Austell

for the publishers

D. BRADFORD BARTON LTD · Trethellan House · Truro · Cornwall · England

introduction

The Scottish Highlands are like no other area in the British Isles—a spacious, unspoiled region of mountains, moors and lochs which has no equal in these islands. The railways of the Highlands, too, are no less unique, being long single-line routes which—apart from the trunk route to Inverness—have the sparse traffic one would expect in such a thinly populated countryside. Since the demise of steam there has not been such a change in the Highland railway map as farther south and over much of this unaltered mileage the single track scene is the same today as it ever was—endless curves, through rock cuttings and along embankments clad with heather or bracken, a landscape of isolated pine clumps, plantations of fir and distant brown or purple moors rising to rock-capped mountains where snow lingers in the north-facing corries until the long midsummer days. The daily work of the drivers on the Highland lines takes them through some of the loveliest and loneliest scenery in Britain; so it did in the days of the K3s and Class Fives, but now in the relative quiet of a diesel cab at the head-end of a train, they see more of the best of Scottish scenery and lineside wildlife—summer and bitter winter—than is realised.

This volume covers the three main rail routes penetrating the Highlands, in the area north and west from Glasgow and Perth and Inverness. First is the West Highland line which runs north from the shores of the Clyde to Crianlarich; thence there is one line westward to Oban and another north—and westward to Fort William and the Mallaig 'extension'. This scenic but strenuous route is the province of diesels from Eastfield depot at Glasgow. The second route is that from Perth to Inverness, the former Highland main line, which runs through the heart of the Grampians. Its gradient profile very roughly consists of two gables, one each more or less towards the northern and southern ends, with a central more level section through Aviemore; the high grouse moors of Perthshire and the Grampians provide a no less scenic setting for this route. In winter it sees some of the most prolonged snowfalls anywhere on BR metals, as numerous illustrations in these pages testify. Third is the line north from Inverness, up through now-busy Invergordon and on the long rambling run to the twin northerly termini of Wick and Thurso. Never a money-spinner in the century since it was opened, this line remained of importance as a vital transport link for the far North of Scotland, as well as for the Orkneys and Shetland Isles. It was a route of strategic importance in wartime to supply men and materials to these northern naval bases. The discovery and exploitation of oil deposits and natural gas in the North Sea has transformed the future for this line, as indeed it also has for the southern link onwards from Inverness to Perth. Third and finally, branching westward from the Northern line at Dingwall, is the Kyle of Lochalsh branch. This serves Skye and the Western Isles, being equally as scenic as the Mallaig line farther south which vies for the same traffic. The discovery of offshore oil may transform the Kyle line—and, sadly, part of the still unspoiled Western Highlands—but it is a branch which to date has had the axe of economy poised over it for some time. Its potential for tourist traffic in summer is considerable, though in winter it is little used. As elsewhere, the problem in increasing tourist passenger traffic is to woo people away from their cars, for the great majority of visitors to the Highlands travel by road. At present, the services to and from Kyle are still scheduled to connect with non-existent steamer services to the Outer Hebrides rather than the tourist trade based on Inverness.

Dieselisation on this section of Scottish Region in the late 1950s was initially a mixed success, with the problems largely confined—on the three main routes in question—to the West Highland. On the face of it the advantages of diesels on the long, far-flung single lines in north and west Scotland were immense—greater power, whether worked singly or in pairs, within existing restricted axle loadings; far longer fuel range; greater ease and centralisation of servicing and stabling—to name but a few. The problem was reliability, on the West Highland line at least, for the class chosen for use was the 61xx series Type 2 diesel-electric built by North British in Glasgow, which proved to be unreliable in service. And on remote lines, reliability is not merely a desirable feature but an essential one.

On the routes to be worked by Inverness-based diesels, to Wick and Kyle as well as south to Perth or beyond, other Type 2s were being tried out in 1958-59. D5511 of the Brush-built A1A-A1A type—later Class 30—was given trials up to Wick (and also to Fort William) whilst D8208 from BTH was also tried out briefly. D5303 of BRCW-build and with Sulzer engine was also received on loan to test its suitability. Results, and driver reaction, to all this indicated the choice of the latter (D53xx series) to spearhead the changeover from steam to diesel out of Inverness. Some were transferred up from Eastern Region—a radical change from working commuter trains out of London to Hitchin or Cambridge—and later deliveries from the works were made direct, incorporating such Highland refinements as fitted tablet catchers from new. By the end of 1962 the transition period from steam to diesel was over at Inverness, with the last of the stud of stalwart Class Fives gone south to work out their time in southern Scotland and in their place some 48 Type 2s. These were a mixture of some 30 of the D53xx Class 26s plus a number of more recently introduced D51xx Class 24s built at Derby. Both had the same Sulzer 6-cylinder (6DLA 28) engine, giving 1160 hp; truly had the Sulzer conquered the Highlands.

Interesting to relate, Inverness drivers, young and old, though they greatly liked the 'Black Fives', took better to their new diesel charges than did other BR depots farther south. Morale was high, with locomotive breakdowns out on the road few and far between. The crews did indeed need to be resourceful in putting something right, for in the Highlands, particularly in winter with blizzards in the offing, a relief locomotive could be a very long way away.

The success of the BRCW-Sulzers at Inverness had not gone unnoticed at Eastfield whose steam locomotives were still coping with the vagaries of the NBL D61xx diesels in the period from 1959-61. In August of the latter year, D5347 and D5348 were tried on the Oban services; these were the 1250 hp (Class 27) versions of the already successful 26s and the upshot was the decision, welcome to Eastfield, that in 1962 they would receive 23 of these new units, to replace steam entirely and to enable the unsatisfactory D61xx to be relegated to other work. Subsequent re-engining of some of these units with Paxman engines was later to improve their ability to spend time out on the road—and not stored or in for repair—but Eastfield men took to their 27s in the manner born. In the mid-1960s Class 25s also arrived at Eastfield

and appeared on occasions on West Highland turns. By 1968 the rest of the Class 27s had all been transferred from LM Region to Scotland, partly to standardise locomotive allocations and to rationalise availability of spares and this confirmed yet again the dominance of the Sulzer engine everywhere in the area here considered.

Since that date in the 1960s there has been little change of note on the diesel scene, for Class 24/25 or 26/27 Type 2s generally dominate all traffic. In the Highlands it may be said that there is great variety of scenery but not of locomotives—except on the Perth-Inverness line which sees wandering Type 4s and others on inter-Regional trains. It is, however, the last place in Britain where one might see a mixed train—out to Mallaig or Kyle—and it was until recently the only locality on BR where one might see triple-headed diesels in daily service.

Class 27 No.5389 again on another train for Glasgow in the same rock cutting as seen opposite, 27 April 1972. Wet rails are still as much of a problem as they were for slipping in steam days and on the succession of sharp curves everywhere on the West Highland it is made worse by overhanging vegetation, as this is no longer 'cut back' as efficiently by the once-common lineside fires which steam locomotives were prone to start.
[P.H. Wells]

The familiar diesel face on the Glasgow - Oban/Mallaig lines of the former West Highland is that of the BRCW Class 26s and 27s, which have provided the backbone of the services for a decade or more following the failure of the Class 22s. On 1 May 1972 No.5389 brings an up train through a cutting on the long climb from Arrochar—four miles or so of 1 in 57/53—to Glen Douglas summit. The line here hugs the eastern side of Loch Long, with striking views westward, and then drops past Whistlefield and Garlochhead to run alongside the Clyde.
[P.H. Wells]

Another of Eastfield depot's Class 27s, No.5365, coasting down the 1 in 53 towards Arrochar with a train of oil fuel tanks for Oban, 2 May 1972. The upper end of Loch Long is on the left.
[P.H. Wells]

The secondman on No.5359 takes the exchanged token at Ardlui with an early morning train from Glasgow to Fort William, 16 October 1972. This station, with its typical broad island platform, is at the upper end of Loch Lomond and for down trains marks the start of the long slog of about fifteen miles up to County March Summit.

[D.E. Canning]

Another view of the train of oil tanks illustrated on the previous page. Two miles or so further on, beyond Arrochar, the line crosses the narrow neck of land dividing Loch Long from Loch Lomond to continue along the west bank of the latter to Ardlui. The problem of encroaching lineside vegetation shows up well in this illustration.

[P.H. Wells]

No.27 104 with the 08.35 Glasgow - Oban on 3 November 1975 in Glen Falloch, approaching Crianlarich.

[T.H. Noble]

At Crianlarich is the junction of the lines to Oban and to Fort William. A feature of the traffic from here are log trains run to and from the big pulp and paper mills at Corpach, near Fort William (owned by Wiggins Teape and built in the early 1960s), which convey block loads of timber from the extensive Forestry Commission plantations hereabouts. No.5355 has charge of a loaded train bound for Corpach, on a day of mist and showers in April 1971. [Derek Cross]

Class 27 No.5360 (still in striped green livery), entering Crianlarich with a pick-up goods, August 1966. The more numerous 27s differ from the 26s in having the slightly more powerful 6LDA28-B Sulzer engine of 1250 hp (1160 hp, Class 26) and GEC instead of CP traction motors. The 26, weighing 77½ tons, has a continuous t.e. of 30,000 lbs and is geared for 80 mph maximum; the 27 weighs 4 tons less, has a rated c.t.e. of 25,000 lbs and 90 mph maximum speed.

[Derek Cross]

Crianlarich, 5 April 1971; Class 27s Nos.5351 and 5369 cross with Fort William - London and Glasgow - Mallaig trains respectively.

[Derek Cross]

In July 1970, a Class 27 pauses at Crianlarich with the morning train ex Queen Street, bound for Fort William. This includes through coaches from Kings Cross, the total journey time from there being 14 hours and 14 minutes. After the Class 22s had been withdrawn, it was rare to see anything except the BRCW-Sulzers on the West Highland; occasionally Class 25s are seen, and DMUs also work regularly to Oban each summer, but since 1961 the 53xx have been the standard motive power in use. The first pair (D5347-48) started on the line in August 1961, working to Fort William, and ran trials out to Mallaig later that year. By spring 1962 they were in command on the Oban services.

[Derek Cross]

Green-liveried D 5361 with an Oban - Glasgow train near Crianlarich, April 1968. This photograph is taken at the very top of Glen Falloch; note the Scots native pines in the background — the last remnants of the ancient Caledonian Forest.
[Derek Cross]

D 5396 with a train at Ach-na-Cloich, about ten miles from Oban, where the line runs close by the southern shore of Loch Etive. The station here, midway between Connel Ferry and Taynuilt, is now deserted and rhododendrons encroach upon the platform and track.　　[C.L. Williams]

Oban, terminus of the Callander & Oban line and southern rail-head for the steamer services that ply in and out of the indented fiord coastline of western Scotland and the Isles; one of the D61xx series of Type 2 diesel-electrics built by North British, D6101, draws away with a train for Glasgow, 20 April 1968. By this date more than half of the 58 NBL/MAN-engined machines that had been built in 1959-60 had been stored or withdrawn due to unreliability, and replaced by Class 27s. Prominent above the station is the mock coliseum which is a feature of the Oban skyline.   [Derek Cross]

D 5352, leaving Oban, takes the sharp curve past the box and into the cutting with a nine-coach train bound for Glasgow (Queen Street), 8 August 1969. This is the standard load for a Class 27, and two bogies more than that of Stanier 'Black Fives' in pre-diesel days. At one stage in the projected changeover from steam the introduction of 2000 hp EE Class 40s was considered on the West Highland lines.

[P.H. Wells]

D5354 entering Oban (at the same location as the facing illustration) with the 08.35 ex-Glasgow (Queen Street) on 21 August 1968. Shunting operations from the quayside wharves alongside the terminus involve some use of the main running lines in this approach cutting. Note that the full headcodes on English Regions are not used on subsidiary services in Scotland.

[P.H. Wells]

Awaiting departure at Oban in the summer of 1962, BRCW Type 2s D5362 and D5361 wait to take out trains for Glasgow and Ballachulish. By this date there were few steam locomotives seen here—chiefly Class 5s on freights or on occasions when there were insufficient diesels to work the summer schedules. The all-conquering Class 27 BRCWs had been cleared for use on the Ballachulish branch, which diverged north at Connel Ferry, displacing steam even there. The increasing number of newly built and ex-Eastern Region 27s available meant not only the end of steam but of the NBL D61xx series, which for a long time had perforce been used in pairs—not only to give more power to keep time but to enable the all too frequent casualties to be hauled in.

[S. Rickard]

A return to Crianlarich and the junction between the Oban/Fort William line: Class 27 No.5402 (now No.27 040) coming over the junction and entering the station with a Mallaig - Glasgow train on an evening in May 1971.

[J.G. Glover]

For up trains, the six-mile climb from Bridge of Orchy up to Tyndrum culminates in 2½ miles which at 1 in 55 is the worst encountered out of Fort William up to this point. The line follows the sloping flanks of massive Beinn Dorian (3524' high) and then Beinn Odhar (2948') after traversing the wide horse-shoe curve of the valley separating these two. Although out of sight this curve is still apparent in this photograph of NBL D6103 with a Mallaig - Glasgow train taken on 20 April 1968. [Derek Cross]

Another mile or so from the previous location D5351 with a Fort William - Glasgow train clears the summit of Tyndrum on 5 April 1971—a scene taken from beside the A82 road. This is the County March (or boundary) which coincides with the summit where the line crosses from Perthshire into Argyll: once over the watershed, it drops towards Crianlarich, through Tyndrum Upper. On the Oban line, on the other side of the valley, is Tyndrum Lower station and the two tracks run side by side down Strath Fillan to the junction at Crianlarich. [Derek Cross]

A down freight headed by the usual Class 27 nears Tyndrum summit from the south, 8 August 1974.   [T.H. Noble]

Class 27 No.27 025, working an up freight from Corpach paper mills, leaves its train at Bridge of Orchy, and backs into the sidings to collect No.27 009 left there overnight after failing on the previous day. The remaining photographs, taken in August 1974, show No.27 025 backing the dead locomotive on to its train and then heading away towards Glasgow with its load of newsprint on sheeted wagons.

[C.W.T. Jamieson]

23

Bridge of Orchy station, April 1971, with D5351 heading home for Queen Street and Eastfield depot with a train from Fort William. The neat and well-built station is typical of the former West Highland. Beyond here, heading north, the line leaves the A82 road which has followed it closely since Ardlui on Loch Lomond and curves away north-eastward to cross the bare upland stretch of Rannoch Moor—mile after mile of bleak moorland and peat bog that is almost uninhabited. [Derek Cross]

Sixteen miles from Bridge of Orchy is Rannoch station, set in the remote heart of the moors, and accessible by road only from the east via the long and meandering B846 — which ends here. A small hotel and the station vie in their claim to be the centre of the hamlet. Here, two crossing Fort William - Glasgow trains enliven the scene on 23 August 1974.   [L. Elsey]

ecember at Rannoch; No.27 016 approaching the station (above) with the 06.00 ex-Glasgow bound for Fort William, December 1975. Below, the same train crossing the viaduct north of the station amid a very wintry landscape.

[T.H. Noble]

August at Rannoch; No.27 001 has the board for the departure with the same train on 22 August 1974. This locomotive was originally numbered 5347 and, as the new class number shows, was the first of the 1250 hp Class 27s to appear. Along with No.5348, she was actually the first to start work on the West Highland line, in 1961. Prominent in the foreground is the granite memorial to J.H. Renton, a director of the West Highland Railway.

[L. Elsey]

Despite bus services and the widespread use of motor cars, the railway is still a vital lifeline in many places in rural Scotland. Here the 06.00 out of Queen Street, unloads mail at Spean Bridge, once the junction for the Fort Augustus branch which extended 24 miles or so north to Loch Ness, but on which passenger services ceased in 1933. Now the station sign proclaims that one should change for the bus service.   [J.A.M. Vaughan]

Class 22 D6103 on a down log train from Crianlarich
at Tulloch on 21 January 1969. Once Eastfield had
received its complement of 23 BRCW class 27s in
1962, the NBL locomotives were relegated to
freights—where their lack of power and unreliability
mattered less—or to periods in store or undergoing
repair. At one stage in 1961, twenty or more were at
St. Rollox works awaiting attention by NBL
staff—with cracked cylinder heads, burned-out
generators and other serious complaints.
Overheating on the up-grades was one basic cause
and Eastfield drivers tended to groan at being
booked for an NBL rather than a BRCW; seasoned
travellers on the West Highland in the nearly 1960s
came to realise that their train would almost
certainly run late if only one locomotive was at the
head. . . From the crew's point of view their good
points were nice warm cabs and a much better ride
than that of a 27. In fairness it ought also to be added
that the Class 22s re-engined with Paxman units
were vastly improved.   [D.E. Canning]

Exchanging the token at Mallaig Junction, entering
Fort William, 22 June 1974.   [D.E. Canning]

The West Highland terminus station at Fort William is crowded into a narrow strip between the town and the waters of Loch Linnhe, as is apparent in these two views in April 1971 (above) and June 1974 (below). There are three short platforms each accommodating six bogies and it is of course necessary for through trains to and from Mallaig to be worked in and out again. To improve matters, a new station has been provided on a more spacious and convenient site at Mallaig Junction, near the site of the former locomotive shed.

[Derek Cross]

The new station at Fort William, 2 June 1976. On the right is No.27004 with the 08.54 to Queen Street and on the left No.27003 with the 09.40 to Mallaig.

[J.C. Hillmer]

The line continuing westward to Mallaig from Fort William was known as the West Highland Extension, a single-line route of considerable scenic beauty opened in April 1901. It was expensive to construct and operate; the first two obstacles facing its builders within a few miles of Fort William were the substantial bridge needed to cross the River Lochy followed by the one required to take the line across the Caledonian Canal at Banavie. This swing bridge is seen here with a westbound train easing across on a June morning in 1975.

[T.H. Noble]

scene on the West
ghland Mallaig
xtension, typical not
nly as regards the
ndscape, with its
ne trees and
eather-clad mountain
opes, but as regards
e neat station
rchitecture and the
ass 27 locomotive:
lenfinnan, July 1970.
his is sixteen miles
om Fort
/illiam—the whole
rty miles of the
xtension being
emarkable for its
evere curvature and
s short but savage
radients, compared
o the preceding run
om Glasgow to Fort
/illiam. There are one
r two brief stretches
t up to 1 in 48 but
othing more than a
ile in length.
[J.A.M. Vaughan]

ond Corpach and
massive paper
s some three miles
m Fort William, the
commences a
el or near level run
ng the north shore
och Eil, parallel to
A880 road. D6129,
a misty evening in
ril 1968, heads a
llaig - Fort William
ked train eastward
r aptly named
heilside station.
[Derek Cross]

Late in August 1973, one span of a bridge collapsed east of Glenfinnan and there was other damage as a result of floods following exceptionally heavy rainstorms and for a matter of several weeks the line was blocked. Nos.5350 and 5359 were isolated, along with twelve coaches, on the down side of the occurrence and they were used to provide a shuttle service between Glenfinnan and Mallaig, with connecting buses laid on to take passengers onwards to or from Fort William. No.5350, photographed from one of these buses at Glenfinnan station, is about to return to Mallaig with its train, September 1973.   [T.H. Noble]

A most interesting feature near Glenfinnan is the long curved viaduct which carries the line over the river flowing down into the head of Loch Shiel. The view down the narrow loch between the mountains is striking, with the tall Jacobite Monument on its shore in the foreground; this view has been made familiar over the years in numerous travel guides and posters. In this scene, D5415—last of all of the Class 27s—eases round the sharp curve with an afternoon train from Mallaig on 15 August 1969. This viaduct was one of the first all-concrete structures of its kind ever built: legend has it that during construction a horse and cart tipping material into one of the piers overbalanced by accident and could not be recovered—remaining in there to this day . . .

[Norman E. Preedy]

A Class 27 threads its way westward near Glenfinnan through the rugged, rockstrewn landscape of the Western Highlands. The line consists of a succession of curves, either in rock cuttings or on low embankments, amid bracken and heather; a sheep by the lineside appears to be the only living thing in sight and the only indication of civilisation are the telephone wires marching alongside the track. On lines such as these, minor rockfalls in the cuttings are not infrequent and when track clearance is limited, the nose-ploughs fitted to the diesels can help prevent too serious a derailment. In February 1974, for instance, No.5381 ran into a rockfall near Glenfinnan and was extensively damaged in the subsequent derailment.

[T.H. Noble]

Mail and newspapers are unloaded at the lonely outpost of Arisaig, next stop but one from Mallaig. The solitary member of staff at the station here combines the duties of ticket collector, signalman, porter and stationmaster. Three up and three down passenger trains pass through each day for nine months of the year and five each way in high summer.   [J.A.M. Vaughan]

For the last mile or so into Mallaig, the railway closely hugs the rocky shoreline and onshore gales in winter when the tide is high can drench a train in heavy spray. In this scene, however, it is summer, as D5408 coasts in with a train from Fort William in August 1969. Mallaig came into prominence as a fishing port in the early years of this century after the completion of the rail link and also served as the port of departure for passenger sailings to Skye and, in the summer, to South Uist and Barra. The principal service is to Armadale, over on Skye.

[Norman E. Preedy]

D5410 and D5408 at Mallaig, August 1969. The railway retains the monopoly of passenger traffic but has now lost entirely the once valuable fish traffic that added revenue to meet operating costs of the long Extension which runs through a region with almost negligible population. In view of the remoteness of Mallaig and the bad, winding roads which reach it, it is a sad reflection upon the competitive ability of BR that road haulage moves away all the considerable tonnage of fish now landed at this busy port.

[Norman E. Preedy]

Stanley Junction, on the Highland main line, some seven miles north of Perth, is where the Inverness and Aberdeen routes used to diverge. On 18 September 1973, Class 47 No.1566 waits by the adverse signal with a Forfar-Perth freight, as two Class 27s— Nos.5327 and 5334—pass the box with a Glasgow - Inverness train. They have a booked time of ten minutes under three hours for the 118 miles from Perth to the Highland capital, including eight intermediate stops. Fastest of the day is the 17.25 ex-Glasgow which has four hours only for the entire run (2 hrs. 40 mins. Perth - Inverness) including the same stops.   [Derek Cross]

No.24 007 going well with another Perth - Inverness freight, passing Ballinluig box on 31 August 1974. Originall
No.5007, and one of the first of the Derby-built Type 2s, she is from Eastfield shed (65A), unlike most of the locals o
this line which are from Inverness (60A) or Haymarket (64B).   [L. Elsey

The morning Perth - Inverness pick-up freight takes the Highland line at Stanley Junction on 18 September 1973 behind Class 25 No.5155. These BR-Sulzer Type 2s (of Class 24 or 25) share the working of the majority of trains with the Class 26 and 27s; both have given first-class service since their introduction. [Derek Cross]

A rare visitor to Pitlochry in April 1969 was Deltic D9019 *Royal Highland Fusilier,* seen here coupled on to Class 27 D5338 with the Perth - Inverness 'Highland Mail'. The Deltic had been specially rostered to work a military special southwards at a later time. With only seven bogies on, some spirited acceleration is recalled by the photographer who travelled on this train.

[Derek Cross]

A pair of Class 25s put out all their combined 2500hp and maximum tractive effort as they accelerate away up the 1 in 85 from Pitlochry on an August day in 1970, heading an Edinburgh - Inverness express. Both are probably from Inverness depot—certainly the leading locomotive, which has the tell-tale spotlights fitted to the 25s that work from there on the far North line.

[L. Elsey]

Class 25 D7503 in a woodland setting near Gary Bridge with a loose-coupled northbound freight, 29 August 1969. Prior to dieselisation, the maximum load permitted a Class 5 on a fitted freight on this route was 28 loaded wagons; the capabilities of the Type 2s was such that it was found this could be increased to a standard maximum of 40 loaded. More or less the only shortcoming of the diesels when they were first sent north from Eastern and LM Regions was their slight deficiency in braking power on the long, steep down-grades when working unfitted freights—a few similar complaints arising later from drivers of 27s on the West Highland line. Adding some fitted stock to the head of loose-coupled trains solved the problem. [L. Elsey]

EE Class 20 No.8030, running light, waits on the up line for a doubleheaded down express from Glasgow to leave Pitlochry, September 1973. These Type I locomotives are now relatively rare on the ex-Highland line, although common on other parts of Scottish Region, but in the early years of dieselisation were regarded as the probable standard motive power for freight duties. Inverness had two in the early 1960s and the five allocated to Kittybrewster (Aberdeen)—which included No.8030—also appeared on the Highland main line from time to time. Their relatively small (400 gallon) fuel tank capacity hindered them somewhat from the point of view of diagramming except over shorter distances, whilst as single-enders they were not as popular with the men. [L. Elsey]

Class 47 No.47 252, passing Dunkeld in August 1974, has a relatively easy load of four coaches and six bogie flats with the northbound Inverness Motorail service. These trains are regularly 47-hauled and also bring other motive power into Perth that is not usually seen locally. Though they have always been frequent in Perth, the first visit of a Class 47 to Inverness was said to be in 1966 with a Motorailer from York. [L. Elsey]

44

Tripleheading on the Highla
main line was not unknown f
time, for loadings were heav
the through services to and fr
Inverness in the summer
months. 'The Royal Highlan
which leaves Inverness for
Euston each evening has be
seen made up to 17 bogies
example. This is five more t
the normal capabilities of a
of Class 24/25/26/27s howev
hard they are driven over Slo
and Drumochter summits a
thus a trio of Class 2s, in
multiple, were rostered for
work. The train here is the 08
Inverness - Edinburgh, seen
near Killiecrankie with a 27
leading the more normal pa
25s, 1 September 1970. Nov
'The Royal Highlander' is ru
two parts at peak periods ir
summer.

[L. El

A northbound express, behind a Class 25/27 combination, enlivens the scene as it passes over the curved viaduct beside the River Garry in the Pass of Killiecrankie. This is one of the most scenic locations along the whole valley which the line follows up into the heart of the Grampians. Beyond Blair Atholl, the scenery changes from the rolling wooded landscape of Perthshire to the bare mountain slopes up by Drumochter summit. At this same point too the real climb begins, with sixteen miles mostly at 1 in 70 against a northbound train. For diesels it is just a full-throttle slog but in the days of Class Fives or their HR 'Castle' predecessors it was a real battle for the footplate crew, and Blair Atholl kept a stud of bank engines in use. [L. Elsey]

09 and D5336 on an
rness - Edinburgh
passing the site of
er Killicrankie
on, on the curve into
tunnel, on 24 August
. [L. Elsey]

ter on the Highland line; Class 40 No.40 113 and Class 24 No.24 107 ease into the crossing loop at Dalanroch with a southbound ght from Inverness on a February day in 1976. Silence descends on the snowy landscape, apart from the faint throb of their nes as they wait . . . Minutes later a whistle in the distance and then a growing roar heralds the coming of Class 47 No.47 206 the well-heated seven coaches of the 13.15 from Edinburgh . . . [D.E. Canning]

The snowbound Highlands in midwinter present a very different face from that which the average visitor sees in summer: deep drifts everywhere, brief hours of daylight, and a lifeless silence that is noticeable. Here Nos.26 042 and 26 044 head south for Perth and Glasgow with the 12.15 out of Inverness at the start of the downhill run from the summit towards Dalnaspidal.

[D.E. Canning]

Two Class 25s with an easy six-coach load amid the vast expanse of moorland near Drumochter (or Druimachdar) Summit, 18 October 1972. The train is the 11.25 Inverness to Perth. This section of line, between Blair Atholl and Dalwhinnie, was formerly double line but is now single; increasing traffic, partly as a result of the greater number of freight trains consequent upon the development of the North Sea oilfield, may result in its being doubled again.

[D.E. Canning]

No.24 107 on the last mile of 1 in 78 to the crest of Drumochter Pass with a northbound freight, 4 February 1976. At one time allocated to Gateshead depot, this is one of the class which is starting to be phased out by DR after nearly twenty years of sterling service. [D.E. Canning]

The signboard alongside the railway at Drumochter Summit, 1484' above sea level, February 1969. The route here is through the upland saddle of Glen Garry which forms the gap through which road and rail negotiate the south-western end of the Grampian range; the mountains on each side rise to more than 3000' and in winter drifting snow is a problem. This is also one of the Scottish 'county marches' (see page 21), the summit being the border between the shires of Perth and Inverness. [D.E. Canning]

Nos.26 042 and 26 040 have a full twelve-coach complement behind them as they sweep past snow-bound Dalwhinnie and its distillery with a train for Glasgow. The leading locomotive is trailing an ominous exhaust which bodes ill for the six miles or so of 1 in 80 that still face them to surmount Drumochter. Both are Inverness-based, being two of the original batch consisting of D5318-5346 which (with Class 25 D5114-5132) had replaced steam on this route by the end of 1962. Inverness drivers acquired a good reputation not only for avoiding breakdowns out on the road but also for putting minor faults right—a self-reliant attitude (very necessary on the remote lines in the Highlands) which was in contrast to the union attitude that prevailed at some depots in England where anything worse than a warning light meant an immediate call for fitters or a replacement locomotive.

[D.E. Canning]

the 09.35 Glasgow - Inverness, behind Nos.26 036 and 26 046 near Drumochter Summit, February 1976.   Below; o.47 550 heading the up 'Clansman' past Dalnaspidal on the same day. This train is a regular Class 47 turn. Class 47s ave put up some notable performances on the route; No.1955, for example, worked a 17-coach special (645 tons) orthbound in 1971 without assistance.

[D.E. Canning]   **53**

Class 27 D5315, with an Invergordon - Glasgow "Cruise Special" organised by the National Trust for Scotland on 18 August 1973, crosses the two-span bridge over the River Spey near Newtonmore. This is at the head of the broad Strath Spey which the line follows through Kingussie and Aviemore.

[Derek Cross]

Newtonmore on 15 April 1969, with D5321 and D5324 in the foreground 'waiting a meet' with D5328 and D5130 on Inverness - Glasgow and Edinburgh - Inverness trains. Architecturally, Newtonmore station is the most attractive on the Highland line. Although Type 2-hauled Highland trains do not carry reporting headcodes, these are allocated in the working timetables.

[Derek Cross]

Class 55 'Deltic' No.9019 *Royal Highland Fusilier* at Aviemore with D5338 on the same train as depicted on page 43 at Pitlochry. Running was so spirited that the train had to wait time at each intermediate stop. This was not the only occasion on which a 'Deltic' has reached Inverness; D9004 *Queen's Own Highlander* was there in May 1964 for a naming ceremony.   [Derek Cross]

More conventional motive power at Aviemore on 30 June 1961, with D5125 on an Inverness train. Built at Derby the previous ye this locomotive (now Class 24/0 No.24 125) was one of the first batch of the class to be allocated to Inverness and is seen here original green livery. Footplate crews took to them even more readily and enthusiastically than they did in pre-war years Stanier's 'Black Fives', which were extremely successful Highland engines.   [Norman E. Pree

With fifteen coaches on, including seven sleeping cars, three Type 2s are needed to handle this train over the Highland main line— Class 27s D5346 and D5342, plus Class 24 D5115; Aviemore, 2 September 1962. To minimise wasteful triple-heading on the heavier trains such as 'The Royal Highlander', a fresh diagram was tried in 1962 which brought a Class 40 up from Perth as a fill-in turn to work this, with a Class 25 or 26 helping out, if need be. Scottish Region had hoped for Class 45 or 46s for the job and in March 1962 D153 was given a trial run from Inverness to Perth with a 17-bogie load. Arrival was a few minutes late, despite some good work. Curiously enough, the otherwise wide-ranging 45/46s have always been relatively rare on the route.   [Norman E. Preedy]

Another scene at Aviemore in the early years of dieselisation, with D5124 and D5125 on 30 June 1961, heading the evening 'Mail' from Inverness. The 75 mph of these 1160 hp Class 24s maximum speed compared with the 90 mph of later BR-Sulzer Type 2s (Class 25s) is no disadvantage on the Highland road. 1961 was the last summer that steam appeared on the route, the few remaining Class Fives from Inverness being then transferred south mainly to Ayr, Stranraer or Carlisle.   [Norman E. Preedy]

Class 26 No.5317 with a Perth - Inverness freight near Aviemore, 14 September 1972. The heaviest freights regularly worked over the route are the Oxwellmains - Inverness cement trains; 18 are the maximum load on this for a Type 2 but normally they are worked by a Class 40 or 47.

[D.E. Canning]

A train from Inverness behind the customary pair of BRCWs crossing Slochd Viaduct near Carr Bridge en route to Perth, February 1969.   [D.E. Canning]

A northbound train crossing the long, curved Findhorn Viaduct, at Tomatin, March 1973. 143' high, this impressive structure of lattice-girder spans on masonry piers is over a quarter of a mile in length (445 yards) and built on a half-mile radius curve.   [W. Collins]

The frozen remnants of a week-old snowfall dapple the brown of the moorland near Slochd summit and form a setting for a southbound train in the winter of 1969. This is the second of the major 'gables' in the gradient profile of the Perth - Inverness route, with the central relatively easy fifteen mile Newtonmore - Aviemore section between them. Slochd is about six miles at 1 in 60/92/70 from the south but much longer, on a ruling grade of 1 in 60, from the north. Indeed it is twenty miles of uphill work, with only two very brief downhill sections, all the way from outside Inverness. [D.E. Canning]

A Class 26 heads a Royal Mail TPO van and a single coach towards Slochd summit *en route* to Inverness on 10 February 1969 — a special train put on as the result of an earlier derailment. [D.E. Canning]

English Electric Class 40s provide an occasional change in the motive power scene on the Highland main line; here, No.40 011 comes through the cutting by Slochd summit with an Edinburgh - Inverness train, 31 January 1976.
[D.E. Canning]

Class 24s head the 6.35 ex-Inverness past the historic battleground of Culloden Moor, 18 October 1972. This is seven miles out of Inverness, where the railway route takes a broad sweep to the north-east to ease the grade somewhat in climbing Drummossie Muir. Then, over the River Nairn, there is half a mile of downgrade but otherwise it is 1 in 60/70 all the way to Slochd, a climb from sea level to 1315' in some 22 miles. Double track extends as far as Daviot, 11 miles from Inverness. [D.E. Canning]

A Class 25 and a 26 start the climb away from Millburn Junction and cross over the single line track to Forres, soon after leaving Inverness, on a Sunday evening in May 1974 with a relief to 'The Royal Highlander'. With sixteen on, including a sleeping car and two mail vans, this would normally have a third locomotive added and there is a lot of sustained full-throttle running ahead for the two Sulzer engines in these Type 2s.

[Norman E. Preedy]

Inverness: No.47 471 awaits departure time of 10.30 with 'The Clansman' for Euston, 20 June 1974. Though they had been visitors for some years (since 1966) the first Class 47s to be allocated to Inverness had only just arrived at this date, with No.47 561 as the pioneer for crew training. [D. Griffiths]

Inverness depot, 20 July 1975; this was rebuilt in the early 1960s from the former HR Lochgorm Works, at the same time that the old—and well known—locomotive roundhouse was demolished and the site cleared. The original allocation here in the early 1960s was 48 Type 2s, two Type 1s and two railbuses (for Aviemore locals and the Speyside branch). [J.C. Hillmer]

The broadly V-shaped terminal layout at Inverness in which trains for Kyle or Wick use the sharply curved platforms on the northerly 'arm' of the V and those for Perth or Aberdeen use the similar but less sharply curved platforms on the south 'arm', makes for time-consuming, and thus expensive, train movements. There is always ample work to be done by the Class 08 station pilots there. One of them marshals the stock of a Glasgow train ready for departure. An interesting feature of working is that to save locomotives being trapped at the buffers and to cut down wasted platform length, some incoming trains are reversed before entering the station, using the triangular layout of the running lines outside the station limit. This was standard practice in steam days.   [A.A. Mackenzie]

One of the large Independent' snowploughs (No.ADB 965198 SC) maintained at Inverness for clearing the lines after snowstorms. This is a regular winter operation in the Highlands and not the exceptional occurrence it is further south. Six of these heavy duty snowploughs were built for Scottish Region at Cowlairs Works in 1963-64 on surplus six-wheel tenders. They can clear 12' high drifts and have proved eminently successful.

[C.W.T. Jamieson]

An early morning scene at Inverness, with Class 24 No.5125 arriving with a freight from the south and Nos.5124 and 5113 waiting for the section with a trainload of pipes from Invergordon; 1 April 1974: Opposite, inside Inverness depot, 31 March 1974.

[Brian Morrison]

Class 26/2 No.5337 at Clachnaharry on 1 April 1974 with the 08.15 Kyle – Inverness. This location, about two miles out of Inverness, is where the line crosses the north end of the Caledonian canal, on a swing bridge similar to that at Banavie at its southern end (see page 31).

[Brian Morrison]

A northbound train from Inverness crossing the graceful masonry bridge over the River Ness soon after leaving the station, 19 September 1973. Below, Class 40 D363 at the same location with train 4E47, consisting of empty grain hoppers from Muir of Ord to Doncaster. This is a regular daily block working to distilleries north of Inverness and is regularly hauled by Eastern Region Class 40s.

[Derek Cross]

Dingwall lies nineteen miles from Inverness through the now closed stations at Beauly and Muir of Ord, and is the junction for the line to Kyle of Lochalsh which departs westward from the northerly line to Wick and Thurso. Here a southbound train, headed by the usual Class 26, departs for Inverness. Parcels traffic remains substantial in the Highlands due to the sparse road services and this is largely responsible for the unsuitability of dmus which might otherwise have seemed well suited to such a route. In fact cross-country dmus were tried on the line but they were not found acceptable, partly on account of lack of power and partly due to their unsuitability in winter—when Highland trains have often to act as their own snowplough. [J.A.M. Vaughan]

In June 1960 passenger services were withdrawn from no less than twenty intermediate stations between Inverness and Wick, leaving open only the principal ones such as Dingwall. This was carried out at the same time as a revision in the bus services serving the same communities, integrating the two modes of transport to cut down the obvious wasteful competition that was taking place. This made a saving of half-an-hour or more on the through journey time, as well as reduced the operating overheads. Journey time of more than six hours in steam days was cut by this, and by the introduction of diesels, to only 4¾ hours. One of the best known of these intermediate halts was Dunrobin, serving the Duke of Sutherland's nearby castle of the same name—now a technical college. In BR days the platform was used as and when required, with trains flagged to a halt by any waiting passengers, until it was closed in 1965. The shed which once housed the Duke's privately owned locomotive and coach is visible in the distance.

[J.A.M. Vaughan]

The far North road is a demanding one in terms of gradients, even though there are no sustained climbs as on the Perth-Inverness line, for a large number of short 1 in 60 or 1 in 70 stretches abound. The route follows the easiest course—the cheapest to construct—and as a result meanders considerably. Over 161 miles of rail extend from Inverness to Wick, even though it is but 80 miles as the crow flies (or 130 miles by road). At Brora, 90½ miles from Inverness, two trains pass on 5 September 1968, D5336 being southbound with a freight and waiting for D5118 to run in with the 11.10 ex-Inverness bound for Wick and Thurso. The recess for the tablet catcher is prominent in this view of the cabside of D5336. The first of the Class 26s to be supplied with these was D5338, in 1960, and later units delivered to Scottish Region had them fitted new.

[Norman E. Preedy]

After running through mile after mile of utterly lonely moorland scenery, rather more level and cultivated country is reached at Georgemas Junction, most northerly junction of all on BR, where the lines to Thurso and Wick divide for the final few miles of the journey. In this scene in September 1973, Class 24 No.5116 has brought an eight-coach train in from the south and, after depositing the two-coach Wick portion beside the signalbox, has drawn forward and back with the coaches for Thurso. The Class 26 working this branch has coupled on and is seen departing round the curve, leaving the Class 24, with a bogie van coupled next to it, to rejoin the Wick portion.   [Derek Cross]

Two further scenes at Georgemas Junction, with D5116 on the return journey, southbound, waiting for D5341 again to bring in the Thurso portion off the branch and attach it to the rear.
[Derek Cross]

Class 24 D5123 shunting a parcel van at Thurso, 4 September 1968. This is the northerly limit of BR metals, 723 miles from Euston, and now a considerably busier terminus as a result of oil exploration in the North Sea off the Shetland Isles.

The twin spotlights fitted to the locomotive (beneath the old-style oval cast 60a shed plate) are needed because of the numerous ungated crossings on this route as well as on the Kyle branch. They are also a help to engine crews in spotting trouble on the track ahead—deep snow drifts, rockfalls, fallen trees, 'wash-outs' and the like. Most of the Inverness Class 25s had them fitted in the mid-1960s but not the 26s. [Norman E. Preedy]

Portrait of a Class 27—D5325 at Wick station, September 1968. The small three-blade snowploughs are left on many Highland locomotives all the year round. In winter they are surprisingly effective and can be relied upon to force a passage through snow a few feet deep. Moreover, they enable the operating authorities to run one of the locomotives fitted in this way light engine back and forth at intervals along a line to keep it open in drifting conditions, thus obviating the use of big independent snowploughs. The only drawback of these loco-fitted snowploughs is that they impede the making of jumper-cable connections necessary to run the locomotives in multiple. There is thus a tendency to run the latter for periods of time either singly or semi-permanently coupled.   [Norman E. Preedy]

D5336 entering Wick, September 1968. Doubleheading on the far North road is unusual, for traffic is not as heavy as south of Inverness. The (weekdays only) service in recent years has been three trains a day each way.

[Norman E. Preedy]

Back at Dingwall, Class 27 D5339 is seen with a Kyle of Lochalsh - Inverness train in the station on 20 September 1963. The station is still well-kept, although by no means as busy as the old days when steam bankers were shedded here to help westbound trains away towards Kyle as far as Raven Rock Summit. The branch has more than once been in danger of closure since the days of Beeching despite its great potential value as a tourist asset to the Highlands. It also forms a vital route-link to the Western Highlands which can be used all the year round.　　　　　[Derek Cross]

Beside Loch Garve, some ten miles west from Dingwall, the branch runs close to the water and alongside the A3 road which closely follows the route of the railway up the valley to Achnasheen: No.26 046 heads towards Dingw and Inverness on a May morning in 1974.

[K.R. Pi

The construction of the Loch Luichart hydro-electric scheme, linked with other nearby lochs, necessitated the raising of the level of the line as well as some diversion of its route. The same train as seen previously, with No.26 046 at its head, is crossing the embankment at the head of the loch, and is passing over the water outlet bridge.

[K.R. Pirt]

A Class 25 with the morning Kyle - Inverness train in May 1974 near Lochluichart where the line runs close beside the loch of the same name. The course of the branch was altered here in the early 1950s, following the extensive hydro-electric scheme in the area.

[K.R. Pirt]

No.24 119 with loaded ballast hoppers for p.w. maintenance is halted at Lochluichart on 25 July 1975, to allow the 11.05 Kyle - Inverness to pass.   [J.C. Hillmer]

Spring comes late to the Highlands, and even at the end of May the trees are barely in full leaf some years: near Loch Luichart, 1974. For scenic beauty the Kyle line rivals the West Highland and for some years in the 1960s one of the former Southern 'Devon Belle' observation cars was used on the route.

[K.R. Pirt]

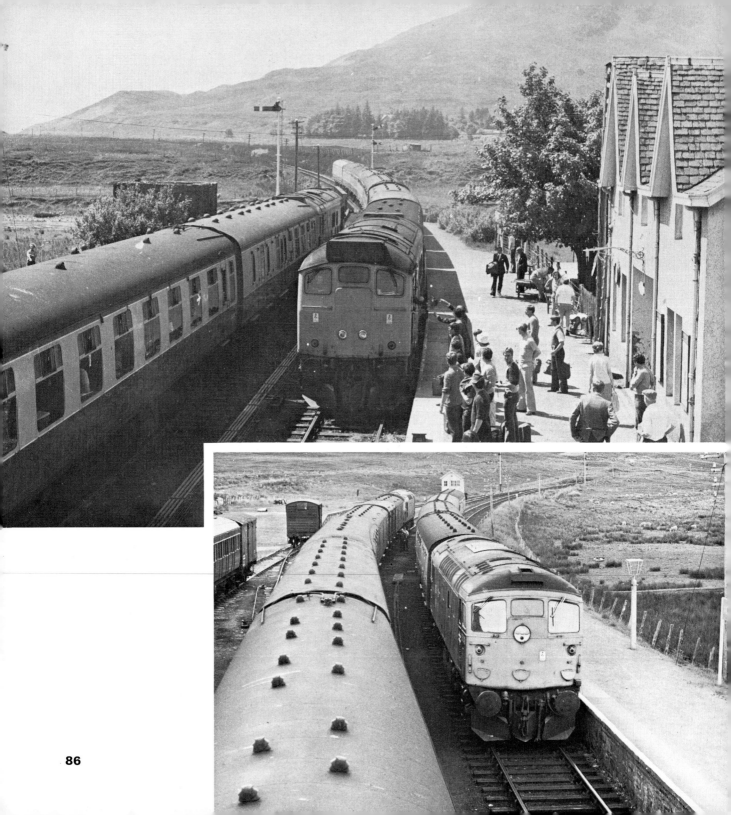

The remote and lonely outpost of Achnasheen sees trains cross twice a day, being one of the few passing loops on the branch. The morning down train from Inverness behind No.24 125 is here waiting to cross with the 11.05 coming in from Kyle (hauled by No.24 129) on 21 June 1974. [D.E. Canning]

An up (Kyle - Inverness) train pulling away from Achnasheen on 18 April 1968. Parcels, mails and light goods traffic to Skye are responsible for the addition of a parcels van or two on almost all trains. Maximum load for a single Type 2 west of Dingwall is rated at 255 tons (eight bogies) and twelve bogies are the maximum permitted over the branch. In practice double-heading is rare, except on specials. [Derek Cross]

Class 26s crossing at Achnasheen; a view from the footbridge looking in the up direction. In the other direction, i.e. westward, the line is still climbing to Luib summit (646' above sea level) another three miles or so away and at that point marks the watershed between east and west; eastward the streams and rivers flow towards Dingwall and the North Sea but westward they all drain into the valley of the Carron which forms the route of the railway down to Loch Carron and the Atlantic shore. [J.A.M. Vaughan]

Class 27 No.5341 with the Inverness - Kyle mixed train, run on Mondays and Saturdays only, near Attadale, 22 September 1973. Below, Class 26 D5336 and Class 24 C5128, in April 1971, at Strathcarron with an Inverness - Kyle freight.

[David M. Cross]

D5339 approaching Strathcarron, the start of the climb to Luib summit, with an up train and (below) Class 24 D5115 and D5132 with a Bristol - Kyle excursion alongside the placid waters of Loch Carron.

[Derek Cross]

Between Attadale and Strome Ferry, the line closely follows the southern edge of Loch Carron, hemmed in by the mountain and sharing its route with the recently constructed B856 road. On this section of about six miles the curves are severe and a speed restriction of 25 mph is in force. Rock slides have occurred and there is a rock shelter at one place, as seen above, shared by twin tunnels for road and rail. The view below is of the Kyle 2K08 'mixed' on 22 September 1973, illustrated earlier.

[David M. Cross]

Class 27 D5330 with four coaches and the inevitable van heads up the shores of Loch Carron on 6 April 1971, the coaches side-lit by the afternoon sun before its rays are overwhelmed by the greyness of a depression coming in from the Atlantic . . . [Derek Cross]

Class 26 No.26 029 on an up train a mile or two out of Kyle at Erbusaig Bay, 15 August 1974. From the rocky shore here there is a superb view across the mouth of Loch Carron to the open sea and the Isle of Skye.   [G.F. Bannister]

Kyle of Lochalsh was a busy little terminus in years gone by and the station is still a bustle of activity at times, as it serves as the principal rail-head for Skye. There is a frequent vehicle ferry service across the mile or so of water to Kyleakin, and motor coaches connecting with the trains. In this exceptionally busy scene in September 1973, a Kyle - Inverness freight is on the left behind a Class 24, with a Class 26 shunting on the goods lines beyond it; on the right are two excursions making ready to leave. These two classes of locomotive dominate the workings on the branch almost exclusively; a stranger seen there in 1973 was a Class 37, on an excursion. [Derek Cross]

D5343 at Kyle on 26 October 1970; without any tourists in the winter months passenger traffic on the branch is very light indeed, three coaches being more than ample. On one occasion in the winter of 1974, when a Class 24 failed near Alladale, a minibus and a car were able to take the entire complement of passengers and crew on to their destination. On this occasion, the locomotive was locked and made secure with its train, and left standing overnight until fitters could arrive from Inverness on a spare locomotive the next day.

[Norman E. Preedy]

No.24 124 awaiting departure for Inverness, 25 July 1975. Journey time for the 82¼ mile run is approximately three hours, with eleven intermediate stops. Nominal speed limit over the branch is 40 mph, with more severe speed restrictions in places and nowhere is there any opportunity for fast running.

[J.C. Hillmer]

A Class 24 shunting at Kyle on 25 July 1975 prior to departing with a freight. The branch retains the lion's share of goods traffic in the area and provides an essential link in the transport network of the Western Highlands. Until some two years ago, the daily goods trains were run only as required. However, oil exploration facilities being developed at Strome Ferry and the transfer of the Naval torpedo research base to Kyle have altered this and freight traffic is now on the increase.

[J.C. Hillmer]

The last glow of the late evening sun picks out the cab details of a BRCW-Sulzer Class 26 in the terminus at Kyle of Lochalsh, by the ferry slip, in the summer of 1974. [D. Griffiths]

STEAM IN ACTION
BR DIESELS IN ACTION
GREAT WESTERN STEAM DOUBLEHEADED
SCOTTISH STEAM IN THE 1920s
LONDON MIDLAND STEAM LOCOMOTIVES
LNER STEAM
SPECIALS
GREAT WESTERN STEAM ON SHED
INDUSTRIAL NARROW GAUGE RAILWAYS IN BRITAIN
in action
NORTH EAST STEAM
MORE SOUTHERN
SOUTHERN STEAM FROM LINESIDE
DIESELS
BR STANDARD BRITANNIA PACIFICS
INDUSTRIAL STEAM
IN ACTION
LONDON MIDLAND STEAM
MIDLAND
GREAT WESTERN STEAM IN ACTION 2
SOUTHERN STEAM
SKIPTON-CARLISLE
MORE BRITISH NARROW GAUGE STEAM
LMSR
STEAM
H.C. CASSERLEY
SOUTH AND EAST
GREAT WESTERN STEAM IN CLOSE-UP
AUSTRIAN STEAM
ELECTRIC LOCOMOTIVES OF THE WORLD
SCOTTISH
MEMORIES OF STEAM AROUND BRITAIN